FRENCH

C000175734

LEARN 35 WORDS TO SPEAK FRENCH

Written by Peter and Helena Roberts

For the first-time visitor to France

An English/French language book, teaching you
how to speak French using 35 selected useful words.

First edition: January 2016

Published in the United Kingdom
by
Russet Publishing
russetpublishing.com

Distributed internationally
by
Lulu *Press* Inc.
Raleigh, North Carolina, USA
lulu.com

Printed version
ISBN   978-1-910537-17-6

Also available as an electronic version

Comments and corrections welcome to
peter.roberts@russetpublishing.com

*"Learn 35 words to speak" is the copyright trade phrase
of Peter and Helena Roberts.*

A WORD FROM THE AUTHORS

This was written by us after many visits to France, with the intention of saving holiday-makers from having to use a phrase book or a dictionary to find words while they are actually trying to talk to someone or ask for help in a foreign country. Impossible!

So we prepared this booklet for absolute beginners, choosing the 35 words that you will need. We have received a good feedback from people who have used our 'Learn 35 words to speak' system.

If you spot errors, or if you want to suggest corrections and improvements, or just to let us know that you have enjoyed our book and that it was useful, please send them to us at:

peter.roberts@russetpublishing.com

Don't forget to learn the 35 words thoroughly *before* your holiday if you possibly can. On the other hand, perhaps it will wile away the time at the airport on your way out, or under a sun umbrella on a hot beach where you can then order your glass of water or lemonade fluently.

Wherever you read it, we are sure that when you have studied it, it will make all the difference to your visit. And remember that a language book will mean more to you and will help you to remember vocabulary if you write notes in it and add your own words and phrases!

Best wishes from Peter and Helena Roberts.

Professional Input. The core French content of this booklet has been checked, corrected, and approved by a professional translation firm using a native-speaking French translator.

CONTENTS

INTRODUCTION

Learn 35 words. Speak French

Yes, really! If you learn the 35 words that this book contains, you will be able to speak more French than you ever thought possible in such a short time! Try it and see. It will work!

Yes, it will take some time to learn 35 words, but it will be worth it the minute you arrive in France and start to speak in French! We'll show you how!

One purpose of the booklet is to help you get around more easily. Although you won't understand what *they* are saying, you will be able to ask for things in restaurants and in the market. You will ask directions, buy tickets, get on a train and arrive at the required destination, and have a good time.

That's why we printed this small booklet - so that anyone who wants to have a holiday in France, and who doesn't know any French, can 'have a go'. With confidence!

Chapter 1 of the book contains the list of 35 words that you will need to know, together with a phonetic guide to their pronunciation. You will find it easy to learn them - make sure you learn them with the correct pronunciation.

Remember that **the pronunciation is very important**. Look at the phonetic part and practise each word faster and faster until it sounds like a single word. So that *la-dis-ee-on* becomes *ladiseeon*, which is, of course, *l'addition*.

The emphasis is equally important. You will notice, that the emphasis is *commonly* on the second-to-the-last syllable of longer words, and often on the last syllable in two-syllable words. That is a good guide.

When you have learned the list and tested yourself thoroughly, you can move on to Chapters 2, 3, and 4, which will show you how to use the 35 words so that you will be understood for most of what you will need on a French holiday.

Why only 35 words?

Because then you won't have to struggle with a phrase book when you want to speak! No waiter, bus conductor, or French citizen is going to hang about while you struggle in a book to find the phrase you want, is he?

We hope that you have a wonderful visit to France, and that upon your return, our little booklet encourages you to have lessons and *really* learn how to speak the language. Good Luck.

Helena and Peter.

Chapter 1

Learn the 35 words.
Here's the magic list.

Unfortunately, there is no other way to learn this list but to sit down and study it for a few days. Our suggestion is that you set aside a regular time each day with someone else - preferably your proposed travel partner - and learn and test each other until you are absolutely sure that you know all of the words and can say their pronunciation correctly without thinking. Then you are ready to move on to Chapter 2.

The List

Don't forget that, in order to help you with the pronunciation, we have given a sort of amateur way of pronouncing each word, and we have underlined the part of the word that needs speaking strongly. i.e. emphasised. Practise until you can say each word quickly, and until you have remembered all of the words.

Correct French pronunciation is not easy, but all you have to do is follow our pronunciation guide as well as you can and you'll be fine. Then simply have a go. Speak it.

1	**a**		un (m)	une (f)
		pronounced:	earn	yune

2	**and**		et
		pronounced:	ay (as in hay)

3	**are**		sont
		pronounced:	sonn

4	**big**		grand
		pronounced:	graun

5	**the bill**		l'addition
		pronounced:	la-dis-ee-on (s as in sock)

6	**a bottle**		une bouteille
		pronounced:	yoon-boot-ay

7	**cold**		froid
		pronounced:	fru-wa

8	**do you have...**		avez-vous ?
		pronounced:	a-vay voo

9	**entrance**		l'entrée
		pronounced:	lawn-tray

10	**excuse me**		excusez moi
		pronounced:	ex-kew-zay mwa

11	**exit**	<u>sor</u>tie (feminine)
	pronounced:	sore-tee
12	**free of charge**	gra<u>tuit</u>
	pronounced:	gra-<u>twee</u>
13	**a glass**	un verre
	pronounced:	earn vare
14	**good evening**	bon<u>soir</u>
	pronounced:	bon-<u>swar</u>
15	**good morning**	bon<u>jour</u>
	pronounced:	bon-<u>jure</u>
16	**hot**	chaud
	pronounced:	show
17	**how much** (is it)?	combien (ça coûte) ?
	pronounced:	com-bee-<u>an</u> (sa koot)
18	**is**	est
	pronounced:	e (as in the word bed)
	is there	est ce qu'il y <u>a</u>
	pronounced:	es-kee-lee-<u>a</u> (useful)
19	**no**	non
	pronounced:	no

20 **one** (1)   un
    pronounced: earn

21 **please**   s'il vous <u>plaît</u>
    pronounced: seal-voo-<u>play</u>

22 **small**   *pet<u>it</u>.*
    pronounced: pu-<u>tea</u> ('pu' as in pup)

23 **station**   gare (feminine)
    pronounced: gar (pronounce the 'r')

24 **thank you**   mer<u>ci</u>
    pronounced: mare-<u>see</u>

25 **that one**   celui-<u>là</u>
    pronounced: sull-wee-<u>la</u>

26 **the** (singular)   le (m)   la (f)
    pronounced: lu (as in lump) la (as in lap)

27 **this one**   celui-<u>ci</u>
    pronounced: sull-wee-<u>see</u>

28 **ticket**   <u>bi</u>llet (masculine)
    pronounced: bee-yay

29 **the toilets** (public)   les toilettes pub<u>liques</u>
    pronounced: lay twal-et poo-<u>bleek</u>

| 30 | **train** | train (masculine) |
| | *pronounced:* | tran |

| 31 | **two (2)** | deux |
| | *pronounced:* | duhh |

| 32 | **I want (would like)** | Je vou<u>drais</u> (polite) |
| | *pronounced:* | ju voo-<u>dray</u> (ju as in jug) |

| 33 | **water (bottled)** | eau miné<u>ra</u>le |
| | *pronounced:* | oh meen-ay-<u>ral</u> |

| 34 | **where? (is)** | où (est) ? |
| | *pronounced:* | oo <u>e</u> (e as in bed) |

| 35 | **yes** | <u>oui</u> |
| | *pronounced:* | <u>wee</u> ('<u>way</u>' is incorrect) |

In French, nouns are either masculine or feminine. This means that there are different words in French for 'the' and different words for 'a'. In English we can just say 'the bottle' or 'a bottle', but not in French.

At this "beginner's level" you won't have time to learn all the details so we suggest that you just try to follow the rule - getting it wrong some of the time. No one will mind.

For the masculine 'the' use 'le' (*luhh*). e.g. le train
For the masculine 'a' use 'un' (*earn*). e.g *un train*
Le train (the train), *un train* (a train).

For the feminine 'the' use 'la' (*la*). e.g. *la gare*
For the feminine 'a' use 'une' (*yune*). e.g. *une* gare.
La gare (the station), *une* gare (a station).

- - - - - - - - oOo - - - - - - - -

So, have you really learned the magic 35 words? Or perhaps not!

If you have not, then go back to the list and keep learning until you can recall the words with no difficulty.

As we said before, learning the list is the hardest part of this job, but it won't take long if you really work at it. The morning time is the best time to learn things - when you are fresh. It's hard work in the evening when you're tired. So, find the first morning that you can - preferably before you go on holiday - and start to learn the list of 35 words. Then re-learn them the day after, and the day after and the day after. Five half hour sessions over five days will be much better than one two-and-a-half hour session. Of course, it's even possible to learn the words while you're on holiday. At least you'll have some time to do it.

If possible, ask a friend to test you, until you are perfect.

Normally, to speak French, you will need about three years of hard effort and a private tutor. Most people don't want to put in that kind of effort or expense. For a first holiday to a foreign country, it's not necessary either. We know, because we've tried it.

On the other hand, it's frustrating on a holiday if you can't speak anything at all, and you feel stupid in a café, at a station, in the city, or when you want to buy something at a countryside stall or in a village shop. So, the following chapters show you how to put 35 words together to speak French!   It's true!

Now that you have learned the magic 35 words, it will take you next to no time to learn how to string them together to say lots of useful things. You will be speaking French in no time at all.

OK! Now we'll show you how to put the words together to speak French!

ADD YOUR OWN NOTES AND NEW WORDS HERE:

....

....

....

....

....

....

....

....

....

....

....

....

Chapter 2
I want something.
Don't we all?

Yes we all want something - mostly all of the time. We need a drink of water - especially in the summer in France.

We need to ask for lots of things like drinks, food, tickets in stations, the bill in a café, and so on.

OK. Believe it or not you already know how to do this!

I want….. It's a very useful statement, but it sounds a bit brusque in English, so we exchange it for the phrase 'I would like to have". That's better! And in French, as in English, we need to use two words - the rather more polite phrase 'Je voudrais'. You want something and it says it politely.   Ju voo-dray (Ju pronounced as in jug)

Je voudrais. Yes - that's it.

What do you want? Lots of things, especially a drink of tea or coffee. You already know the word for tea - we didn't have to put it on our list. It's *thé* (pronounce like tay). So - I want tea.   Je voudrais du thé. (Here 'du' is pronounced exactly like the English word 'dew'.)

That's it. Not very sophisticated, but it says it all doesn't it? You can order some tea in a cafe already. And they will understand what you want. You'll get some tea.

There is also coffee (café), pronounced *ka-fay*, black (noir pronounced *nwar*) or white (blanc pronounced *blonk*).

So let's add the word 'du' and make it sound more civilised.

Je voudrais du café.
I want some coffee.

And to top it off and make it sound even more polite, we add the words for 'please' - *s'il vous plaît*. The pronunciation for which is given in our list of 35 words.

Je voudrais du café s'il vous plaît.
I want some coffee please.

Je voudrais un verre d'eau s'il vous plaît
I want a glass of water please.
(You pronounce the joined up words *d'eau* exactly like the English word *dough*.)

Je voudrais un café noir s'il vous plaît.
I want a black coffee please.

C'est bon. (pronounced *say bon*)
This is good.

Je voudrais une bouteille d'eau gazeuse minérale s'il vous plaît. (gazeuse means with gas - sparkling - and is pronounced gaz-uuz)
I would like a bottle of sparkling mineral water please.

If you don't want your water fizzy, that's easy too. You don't have to try to think up an equivalent phrase for the English words 'still water', you just say "Pas gazeuse", which is pronounced pa-gaz-uuz.

In fact, there's another useful tip for every situation. If you know one adjective, but don't know it's opposite word, just add the phrase n'est pas' pronounced neh-pa. For example, you want to say that something is warm, but you can only remember the word 'froid' meaning cold. You can complain: *'Celui-ci n'est pas froid'*. This is not cold. Or 'This is not good': *'Celui-ci n'est pas bon'*.

Je voudrais une limonade s'il vous plaît. *(lee-mon-ad)*
I want a lemonade, please.

Je voudrais l'addition s'il vous plaît.
I want the bill please - in the restaurant or bar. Perhaps you actually don't, but someone has to!

That's it - you are in control of the situation in the cafe. But don't forget 'please - *s'il vous plaît*, and 'thank you' - *merci*.

ADD YOUR OWN NOTES AND NEW WORDS HERE:

....

....

....

....

....

....

....

....

....

....

....

....

Chapter 3
To find something.
We often need to find places.

We all need to find something - mostly all of the time.
We need to know where to get a train, or a taxi, or where to
buy a paper or a stamp. We need to find the right train. We
need to find a garage. We need to ask for lots of things.

Most commonly, in our experience, we need to find the
ladies or gents toilets.

No problem. You already know how to do this from your
list of 35 words. You did say you'd learned them didn't
you?

Où est 'where is'   *or*   *Où sont* 'where are'. It's pretty
easy.

Où sont les toilettes, s'il vous plaît ? *Where are the toilets,*
please? Which, politely asks for the public toilets in a café.
It's not worth learning the words for male and female
because 99% of toilet doors in public places have a symbol
of a man or a woman on them - standard all over the world.
You'll see which door is right for you when you get there!

Où est la gare ?
Where is the station?

(By the way, below, *Où est un* is pronounce, *oo et earn,* and *Où est une* is pronounce, *oo et yune*)

Où est un taxi? Taxi is pronounced the same as in English.
Where is a taxi ?
*(*Pronounced *oo et earn taxi ?)*

Où est une banque ? …un café ? …un café Internet ?
Where is a bank?   …a cafe ?   …an internet cafe ?
(*Internet* is pronounced *ann-tur-net.*)

Où est l'Hôtel Hilton ?
Where is the Hilton hotel?

Où est un docteur ou un hôpital ?
Where is there a doctor or a hospital ?
(pronounced oo et earn *dok-tur oo earn op-i-tal.*)

Anyone who speaks fluent French will tell you that the above sentences are basic. But they will work! That's the main thing. You have the option of standing in the town square like a goldfish with your mouth opening and closing and nothing coming out, or you can say something that is not grammatically perfect, but gets you what you want. It's an obvious choice!

ADD YOUR OWN NOTES AND NEW WORDS HERE:

....

....

....

....

....

....

....

....

....

....

....

....

ADD YOUR OWN NOTES AND NEW WORDS HERE:

....

....

....

....

....

....

....

....

....

....

....

....

Chapter 4
To buy something.
Don't we all want to do that?

Yes we all want to buy something during our holidays - mostly all of the time. We need to buy presents, food, tickets, papers, postcards, etcetera.

So we could try to teach you a list of a hundred different things that you might want to buy. However, to save you the trouble most of the time, you can learn two words that will stand in for nearly everything: 'this', and 'that'.

Nonetheless, if you're smart, you'll buy a small, English/French/English pocket dictionary from your local bookshop before you go abroad. Then you'll have a list of thousands of things that you can ask for.

Ultimately, of course, you can use your finger to point to something when you want it.

I want this! or I want that! It's easy in English - and in French

You learned the words on the list so...

Je voudrais celui-ci. (I would like this) or Je voudrais celui-là, *s'il vous plaît.* (I would like that, please).

It's easy. Now you can ask for anything in the world that you can actually see at the time. I want to buy this or I want to buy that. Just point to it. What could be easier?

If you want to look up words, then that is also fine. For example, you might want to look up the word for a postcard, or a stamp, and then ask for them in the shop, because you might not be able to see a stamp to point to.

If you look up the word for stamp in a dictionary, you will find that it's called a '*timbre*'. It is masculine and therefore is '*un timbre*'. (Pronounced *earn tam-bruh*)

So you walk up to the counter in the shop/post office and say: *Je voudrais un timbre, pour le Royaume-Uni, s'il vous plaît.* (ro-why-ome-you-knee) It is simple but they will understand you! "I would like a stamp for the United Kingdom". And don't forget to be polite with "s'il vous plaît".

Before you buy something, you may wish to check how much it would cost. So you need the word '*combien?*' from the list of 35 words that you learned. Just use it with '*ça coûte*' to make '*combien ça coûte?*'. It means *'how much does it cost?'*

Or to be a bit more adventurous, you could say: Combien *ça coûte, celui-ci?* How much does it cost, this?

Or when you have bought something, you could say, Combien *ça coûte, celui-la?* How much does it cost, that?

Of course you don't know enough French to understand the number they say back to you, which is a kind of problem, but we found that you can often see on the electronic till how much the thing is if you are buying it, or ask them to write it down by using hand signals if you haven't yet bought it. It works a treat. Everything is in Euros, so they write it down and you understand! That's fairly easy!

A bit of a tip: we suggest that you carry around a very small notepad and ball point pen with you, so that you can ask people to write things down for you - such as the price of goods before you purchase them.

ADD YOUR OWN NOTES AND NEW WORDS HERE:

....

....

....

....

....

....

....

....

....

....

....

....

Chapter 5
To speak French.
Your dream.

You wanted to speak French when you bought this book.

Well now you can. With just the 35 words we have taught you, you can speak an awful lot.

You won't believe it until you try, but you can get by for an entire holiday. And, if you have bought a small dictionary, you will learn another 35 words while you are away and you will be well on your way. You might even go to classes back home and improve more. Who knows?

Anyway, here are some of the things that you can now say that you never thought you would.

Je voudrais un café décaféiné.   (day-caffay-nay)
I want a decaffeinated coffee.

Je voudrais thé pour deux.
I want tea for two.

Où est la gare s'il vous plaît?
Where is the station please?

Où est le train pour Paris?   (Pronounced *pour Pa-ree*)
Where is the train for Paris?

Combien *ça coute, celui-ci? Cette carte ?*
How much is this? This card ?

Je voudrais l'addition s'il vous plaît.
I want the bill please.

Je voudrais un café et deux verres de limonade s'il vous plaît.
I want a coffee and two glasses of lemonade please.

Ex<u>cus</u>ez moi. Où est l'Hotel Majestic, s'il vous plaît?
Excuse me. Where is the Majestic hotel, please?
(l'Hotel is pronounced low-tell.)

You get on a bus and ask the driver or passengers 'Ex<u>cus</u>ez moi. Pour Par<u>is</u>?' (*Excuse me. For Paris?*) Simple. They will either nod and mutter 'oui' or say 'non' and point you in the right direction. We have done this and it works.

Où est un taxi, s'il vous plaît?
Where is a taxi please?

Je voudrais une bière.
I want a beer. (pronounced *yune bee-air.*)

There is red wine (*vin rouge*), pronounced *van rooj*, or white wine (*vin blanc*), pronounced *van blonk*)

Je voudrais un verre de vin rouge.
I want a glass of red wine.

Je voudrais une bouteille de vin blanc.
I want a bottle of white wine.

Don't you think that this is great? You have learned 35 words (plus one or two more sneakily) and you are speaking French on your holiday. Well done!

And there are plenty of pages throughout this booklet where you can add your own new words. Soon you'll know a lot more than 35!

We hope you are as pleased as we were when we wrote this little book for ourselves, on holiday in France.

Please remember that what you have learned here is very basic and is just a start. To speak French well, you need to read proper textbooks and go to classes with a good teacher. Or even get private lessons. We hope we have given you the incentive to do so.

But if you don't study the language more deeply, you can always take our booklet with you when you go to France again!

With best wishes,
Peter and Helena Roberts.

30601195R00020

Printed in Great
Britain
by Amazon